9/21/99

grade 3-4

A HOME FOR LADY LIBERTY

CONTENTS

NOTE: Glossary words are **boldfaced** the first time they appear in the text.
🐾 Paw Print Notes provide additional information.

y name is Jackson. Jackson B. Hill the Twenty-fourth, to be exact. I live inside the Statue of Liberty in New York City, but I'm not the first mouse to live here. My great-great-great-great-great-GREAT grandmother, Sophie Du Bois (pronounced Dew-**bwa**), came to America from France over a hundred years ago and lived in this very room.

We mice know a lot about the Statue of Liberty; we've learned about it in school. We know about Monsieur* Laboulaye (Mehs-**yer** Lah-boo-**lay**), whose idea it was to give the **monument** to America. We also learned about Monsieur Bartholdi (Bar-**tol**-dee), who designed and built the statue. But there was someone else who was there to see the statue grow from an idea into an international symbol of freedom. Can you guess who it was? Right! My **ancestor**, Sophie Du Bois. This is her story.

Sophie was born in 1859 in a big house just outside of Paris, the capital of France. She and her ten brothers and sisters, along with their parents, lived in a mouse hole in the kitchen. Of course, with that many mice in it, the hole was crowded and noisy. Sophie would escape to the quiet library, where she could read Monsieur Laboulaye's books. He was the master of the house.

*Monsieur—the French word for Mister.

People from many cultures live and work together in New York City but still take pride in their own national customs. Still today hundreds of thousands of **immigrants** from all over the world arrive in America to begin new lives.

One day, as Sophie was curled up on the rug reading, Monsieur Laboulaye himself stepped on her tail. She let out a frightened squeak as he plucked her off the rug. Spying the book, he exclaimed, "An educated mouse, *mais oui*,* the very best kind to have. Keep up the reading, young lady!" And with that, he placed her gently on the carpet, where she scurried away, flushed with pleasure from his praise.

From then on, Sophie greatly admired Laboulaye and would stay up way past her bedtime to listen to him and his friends talk about America and the **principles** of **democracy** and **liberty** found there. She was a smart mouse and understood everything they said. Well almost everything.

One night she heard Laboulaye and a man named Bartholdi discussing an amazing idea—they wanted to build a huge statue that would be given as a gift to America from France. Having learned all about America from Laboulaye, Sophie thought this was a splendid idea.

mais oui (may wee)—French for "definitely yes".

Laboulaye and his associates would often gather in his **salon** to discuss their dream of democracy. Laboulaye even wrote two books about the subject. In this illustration he is standing and Bartholdi has his arms crossed. When Laboulaye first conceived of the statue in 1865, France was ruled as a **monarchy**. By the time Lady Liberty was dedicated in 1886, France had become a republic and was ruled democratically.

France was America's first official ally.

Soon Monsieur Laboulaye was spending almost all his time raising the money needed to build the statue. As Laboulaye's friend, Sophie also worked hard to help make his dream come true. She collected spare change, made sketches of the statue, and visited the workshop where Monsieur Bartholdi had finally begun work on the great monument.

Sophie was fascinated by the creation of the statue, which she named Lady Liberty. Monsieur Bartholdi and the workmen were soon accustomed to seeing her furry little face peeking over the edge of the copper sheets used to make the statue, or scampering about with a **rivet** between her teeth. As the years went by, Sophie's brothers and sisters married and found homes of their own, but Sophie wanted to stay near Monsieur Laboulaye and Lady Liberty.

Then one night Sophie was startled awake by thumping on her door. She opened the door to Monsieur Fromage (Fro-**mahj**), her neighbor from a mouse hole in the pantry. Monsieur Fromage stroked his whiskers mournfully and said, "I'm sorry to wake you at this hour, my dear, but I'm afraid I have some bad news."

He had come to tell her that Monsieur Laboulaye had died. Sophie was heartbroken.

Before building the actual statue, Bartholdi started out making small models that grew successively larger. His final model, made of plaster, was one-fourth the intended size of the statue. It was taken apart, and by using precise measurements, each piece was enlarged to full size.

The **artisans** who created Lady Liberty used very simple hand tools, including giant hammers called mallets and carving tools called chisels. Electric tools did not exist at the time.

Without Monsieur Laboulaye, Sophie felt terribly alone. She was very sorry that her friend would never see Lady Liberty completed. It was this thought that gave Sophie an idea—a scary idea, but one she knew she must try to accomplish. As soon as the statue was finished, she herself would travel with it to America. Although Laboulaye wouldn't see Liberty standing tall and proud in her new home, Sophie would be there. She did not know how far away America was exactly, but she knew that the voyage would take many weeks.

Because the statue was not yet done, Sophie had plenty of time to say goodbye to her family and friends. It is not an easy thing to leave your loved ones behind, but Sophie was truly excited about starting a new life in America. At last the big day arrived. Liberty was taken apart, packed into many crates, and carried aboard the ship *Isère* (Ee-**sair**). Inside one crate was a tiny stowaway, Sophie.

The passage across the Atlantic Ocean was rough and stormy. Sophie could hear the waves slapping against the boat and men shouting above deck. The rocking motion of the ship made her head spin and her stomach queasy. Perched inside Liberty's ear, Sophie felt cold and frightened in the dark. But she was comforted by the statue's familiar face.

The *Isère* was a French naval **frigate** that was used as a cargo ship for the statue. It set sail for New York in 1885. Most immigrants made the four-week crossing of the Atlantic Ocean on passenger steamships. For the majority of immigrants, conditions on the overcrowded boats were unbearable, but they endured in the hope of a better life in America.

When the *Isère* finally pulled into New York Harbor, Sophie stared wide-eyed at the city that she would call home. As workers began unloading the crates that held the pieces of the statue, Sophie said a silent goodbye to Lady Liberty, vowing to be the first mouse to see her when she was put back together again.

Making her way into the city, she was overwhelmed by the noise and all the people. She noticed cats, dogs, and birds from all over the world, dodging traffic, and looking as if they were very busy indeed. Everywhere she turned, the sound of strange languages met her ears. For a moment, she felt afraid. " How will I ever make new friends?" she wondered.

Sophie needn't have worried. She soon found a little hole in a hat shop, made new friends, and learned English. Of course she scoured the papers for news of Liberty, which had remained packed in her crates until a **pedestal** could be built for her. Over a year passed before Sophie finally heard the announcement—the tremendous task of anchoring Liberty onto her new pedestal was nearly complete.

11

As she had promised, Sophie was the very first mouse to see Lady Liberty put back together again and standing tall on her own island in New York Harbor. When the whole city turned out to welcome Lady Liberty with speeches and cannon fire, Sophie threw a party of her own. She invited her new friends and put out plenty of sparkling French cider and cheese—for it is true that mice are quite fond of cheese.

As she gazed at the circle of happy faces, the memory of Laboulaye brought a tear to her eye, and she raised her glass in a silent toast. "We did it," she said quietly to herself. From now on Lady Liberty would stand as an inspiration to the whole world.

Sophie and her friends are dressed in national costume to pay tribute to their **cultural heritage** and to the freedom they all have to live side by side in peace. Joining our French mouse are a mallard who **emigrated** from Holland, a cat with Swedish heritage, and a Kerry Blue Terrier from Ireland.

Over a million people attended the dedication celebration, which lasted for several days and included fireworks and a tickertape parade in New York City.

Bartholdi had chosen Bedloe's Island as Liberty's home more than 15 years before her dedication. In 1924, the island was renamed Liberty Island.

EMMA LAZARUS

Emma Lazarus wrote this famous poem which is inscribed on a plaque inside the pedestal at the Statue of Liberty. In the fall of 1883 Emma was asked to write a poem for a literary **auction** arranged by the American Committee for the Statue of Liberty. The committee wanted to raise money to help build a pedestal for the statue.

Emma was Jewish and at the time she lived, the Jews in Russia were treated very badly. They were targets of violence and hatred. In order to get away from this treatment, hundreds of thousands of them left Russia. Many of these people made their way to the United States. Emma Lazarus met some of these **refugees**, and she was touched by their stories.

When she wrote her poem, called "The New Colossus," Emma remembered how the Russian Jews talked about freedom, something she and other Americans sometimes took for granted. Her words captured the spirit of hope and longing for freedom that the Statue of Liberty has come to symbolize for **oppressed** people all over the world.

The New Colossus

Not like the brazen giant of Greek fame,
With conquering limbs astride from land to land;
Here at our sea-washed, sunset gates shall stand
A mighty woman with a torch, whose flame
Is the imprisoned lightning, and her name
Mother of Exiles. From her beacon-hand
Glows world-wide welcome; her mild eyes command
The air-bridged harbor that twin cities frame.
"Keep, ancient lands, your storied pomp!" cries she
With silent lips. "Give me your tired, your poor,
Your huddled masses yearning to breathe free,
The wretched refuse of your teeming shore.
Send these, the homeless, tempest-tost to me.
I lift my lamp beside the golden door!"

What's liberty to you?

For a better understanding of Emma Lazarus' strong feelings, read this poem out loud. Then write a poem that tells how you feel about America.

Hey kids, ready for a guided tour of Lady Liberty? Let's kick it off by flipping over the page to see an exterior, or outside, view of the statue. There are lots more things to learn and to do in the next part of the book, so let's go!

The Lady's torch is gilded in 24-karat gold leaf.

Her right arm is 42 feet long.

The seven points of Liberty's crown symbolize the seven continents and seven seas.

Her skin is green because copper, as it weathers, turns from reddish-brown to patina green, also called verdigris.

The diameter of her waist is 35 feet around.

Liberty's face is ten feet wide, and each eye measures two feet six inches across.

Lady Liberty's face bears a resemblance to Bartholdi's mother, and her strong arms are said to be modeled after those of his wife, Jeanne-Emilie.

Her tablet reads, in Roman numerals, "July 4, 1776," the day the United States declared independence from Great Britain.

The statue's skin is made of 300 sheets of copper, each about $^1/_{10}$ of an inch thick.

Liberty rises to 151 feet from her base to the top of her torch. With the pedestal, she stands just over 305 feet—that's about 30 stories high.

On October 28, 1886, the statue was formally accepted on behalf of the American people by President Grover Cleveland.

INSIDE LADY LIBERTY

The Statue of Liberty is a hollow structure. Four wrought iron posts held together with horizontal and diagonal supports form the central tower. Branching out from the central tower, roughly in the shape of the statue, is a secondary framework.

This framework, which is made up of hundreds of thin, flat iron bars, is very flexible. The flexibility of the secondary framework allows Liberty's copper skin to expand and contract in response to heat and cold. It also enables the statue to move with the wind. Liberty can sway up to three inches, and her torch can move up to five inches.

BRAIN TEASERS

NOTE: The answers to all these questions can be found throughout the book. They are also in the back of the book.

1 On what date was Lady Liberty officially presented to the American people?

2 Why is the statue's skin green?

3 How many points are on Liberty's crown and what is their significance?

4 What was the original name of Liberty Island?

5 How many pounds of copper did it take to make the statue's skin?

6 Including the pedestal, how tall is the Statue of Liberty?

7 How many steps in the statue? How many in the spiral staircase to the observation deck?

8 Who wrote the poem that is inscribed on a plaque inside the pedestal of the Statue of Liberty?

9 Who designed the special construction method used to construct the statue?

10 How many people visit the Statue of Liberty each year?

Are you ready to tackle
more fun stuff? Flip over the page
for a cross section of the statue that shows
what she looks like on the inside. Then see
how you score on the rest of the tricky
brain ticklers in this section.

A wrought iron
tower measuring
40 feet supports
Liberty's torch arm.

Wrought iron posts.

Secondary framework.

Central tower is
nearly 97 feet tall.

Copper outer covering.

The 25 jewels in Liberty's
crown are actually windows.

Lady Liberty is visited by
more than 3,000,000
people every year from
all over the world.

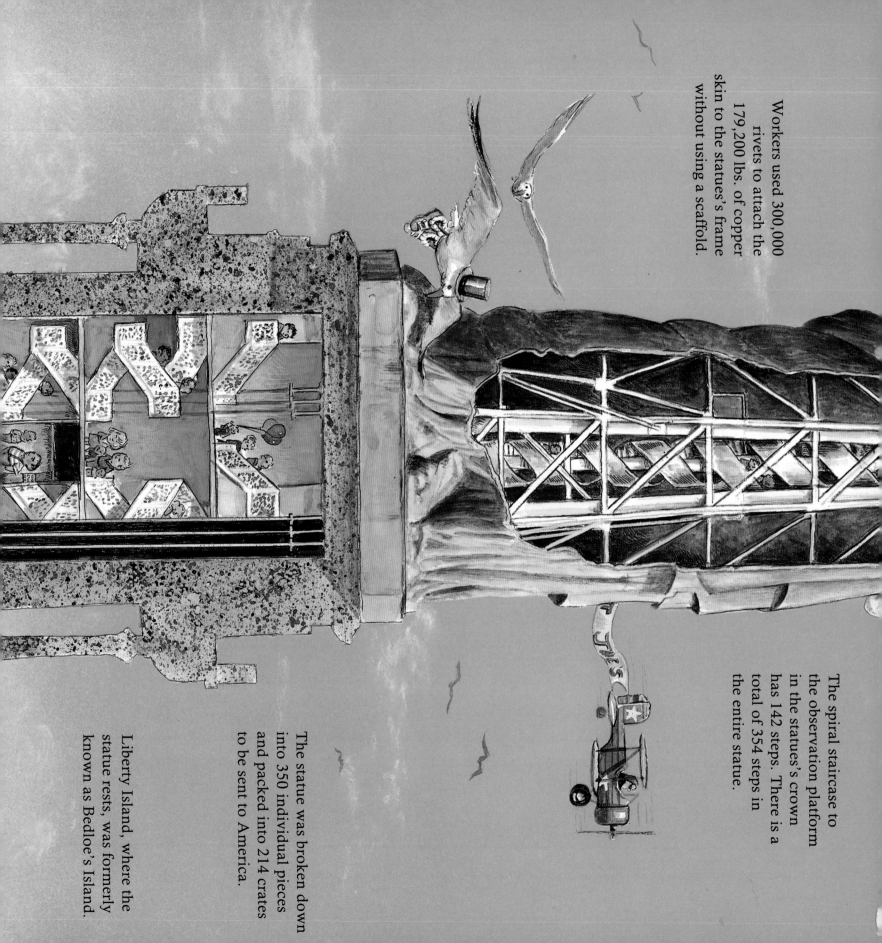

Workers used 300,000 rivets to attach the 179,200 lbs. of copper skin to the statue's frame without using a scaffold.

The spiral staircase to the observation platform in the statue's crown has 142 steps. There is a total of 354 steps in the entire statue.

The statue was broken down into 350 individual pieces and packed into 214 crates to be sent to America.

Liberty Island, where the statue rests, was formerly known as Bedloe's Island.

WHO IS LADY LIBERTY?

These paintings are on display at the Statue of Liberty. They show Libertas—the Roman goddess of Liberty. She looks a lot like Lady Liberty, don't you think?

For most of us, freedom means being able to choose where and how we will live our lives. Grandma Sophie told our family that Monsieur Laboulaye believed people could be free and live in harmony if everyone worked cooperatively and obeyed the laws that had been made by the people. He intended Lady Liberty to be a peaceful symbol of that freedom—lighting the way for the people with her torch.

KEEP THE PEACE GAME

(Solution in back of book)

Sophie once heard Monsieur Laboulaye state: "Liberty lives only through truth, justice, reason and law." Even in a society based on freedom, law and order must exist or conflict will grow out of control. Conflict is a natural thing—everybody encounters conflict sometimes. But to keep the peace, it helps to have someone in charge to make sure goals can be achieved in a fair way.

These three animals and their lunch all need to make it from Battery Park to Liberty Island for their picnic beneath Lady Liberty's comforting shadow. As long as they are all together, everything is fine. The problem is that the dog needs to carry the cat, the mouse and the cheese on his back as he swims across the harbor, and he can take only one at a time. If the cat and the mouse, are left alone together, the cat will chase the mouse. If the mouse and the cheese are left alone together, the mouse will eat the cheese. Can you figure out how he gets them all to Liberty Island safely in seven crossings? (One crossing equals one way.) Use coins to make your moves.

Just think . . .

* What does freedom mean to you? If you could do or be anything you wanted, what would it be? How would you feel if someone told you that you couldn't be or do what you wanted? Would you just give up?

* Imagine you and a friend had to live in a small house together for one week. Work together to make a list of rules to live by for that time. How would your rules be different, and would you be able to live by each other's rules?

* What are some freedoms you have that other kids in the world don't? Would you welcome a new kid from a faraway, strange place? How could you help him or her to belong?

IMMIGRATION

Many immigrants arriving in the 1800s were children. These kids then grew up side by side. A lot of them eventually married other Americans with different national back-

grounds. In this way, people gained better understanding of their neighbors. And that is still happening today, more than ever!

■ What is your own cultural or national heritage?

■ Family **heirlooms** remind us of our ancestors' former homes. My Grandma Sophie left our family her kerchief-shawl that I use as a rug in my apartment in Lady Liberty. What heirlooms have been passed on in your family? What things would you like to pass along?

It is a very narrow and steep spiral stairway to the crown of Liberty. If you climb these 142 steps you'll be among the millions of others who have viewed New York City from the crown's windows.

Here's a closer look at how Liberty's skin was formed. Wooden frames were shaped around plaster models. Then copper sheets were hammered into the frames with mallets. This process is called repoussé.

HOW WAS LIBERTY BUILT?

The task of assembling Lady Liberty was very dangerous, which made it quite remarkable that not a single person died during the process. By comparison, the construction of the Brooklyn Bridge, another complex project that was completed in 1883, cost at least 20 men their lives.

■ Did you know that Lady Liberty's skin is made of copper, the same metal from which pennies are made? I figured that it would have taken close to 29 million pennies (that's worth $290,000!) to make her skin.

■ And that's just the copper. The Lady's skeleton is built of steel posts and bars weighing close to the number of kids that it would take to fill about 140 classrooms.

■ Rivets were used to anchor Lady Liberty's skin to the skeleton. If you placed each rivet one in front of another, the trail of rivets would be about three miles long.

■ Liberty's crown was made to look as if there were jewels inset, but they are actually windows.

*Liberty's original torch is on display in the main lobby of the statue. It used to be lit up at night like a lighthouse beam but it never worked very well. Today Liberty holds a **gilded** flame— just the way Bartholdi envisioned it.*

STICKS, STICKS, STICKS

(Solution in back of book)

The Statue of Liberty was constructed in pieces, which allowed it to be broken down and packed into crates for its journey to America. After the pedestal was completed, the statue was put back together like a gigantic puzzle.

The following puzzles can be made with twigs, straws, toothpicks, or some other small straight item—all of the same length. In altering certain shapes, you're using your mind like a problem-solving engineer!

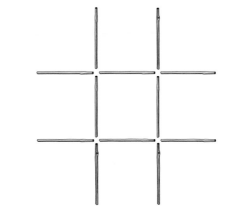

Use 12 sticks to make this design. Then, by moving three of the sticks, create three identical squares touching each other.

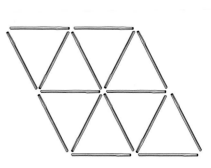

Use 16 sticks for this design. Remove four sticks in order to leave four identical triangles.

LIBERTY'S 100TH BIRTHDAY

Lady Liberty belongs to the American people, and it's our responsibility to take care of her. If I see a bolt that needs tightening, I do it. If there's a piece of trash left behind by a visitor, I clean it up.

In 1985 Lady Liberty turned officially 100 years old. Between 1982 and 1985, Americans donated $69,000,000 to help restore the statue to her former glory. Like any 100-year-old, she needed some help!

Much work was done to bring the Lady back to her original strength and beauty. For example, all of Liberty's ribs were replaced, her crown was rebuilt, and she was given a brand new torch.

Liberty's copper skin was in good condition and required very little repair. This was largely from the protective **patina** that forms on the copper surface.

21

HOW BIG IS LIBERTY?

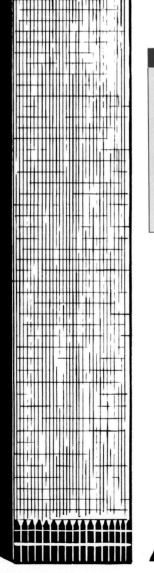

WORLD TRADE CENTER

The Trade Center towers in New York City are each a gigantic 1,350 feet tall. Wow, it would take about four and a half Liberty monuments to match that height! Of course, these buildings are much younger, having been completed in 1970. The elevator ride is one of the fastest in the world and will take your breath away.

EIFFEL TOWER

The Eiffel Tower stands about 984 feet in Paris, France. Besides being a great place to get 360-degree views of the city, it is also used to transmit television signals and houses meteorological equipment for weather predictions. It took only two years to build and was completed in 1889.

When the Statue of Liberty was built, it was the largest sculpture of its time. In Europe, sculptors like Liberty's designer Frederic Bartholdi were in the habit of thinking big. Americans attached more value to bridges and buildings, but it didn't take long for the Americans to construct towering wonders themselves, such as the Washington Monument, which opened in 1888 in Washington, D.C.

Bridge builder Gustave Eiffel not only designed the Eiffel Tower, but also invented the construction method used for the Statue of Liberty ten years before that. His skeleton design of iron posts and straps allowed for some of the largest structures built in that period. The size of any structure, including the human being, relies on the size and strength of its skeleton.

Compare the sizes of the structures shown here and look at the dates they were built. Technology sure has changed in the last hundred years. But even thousands of years ago, the pyramids and the Great Sphinx of Egypt were constructed out of stone by thousands of men working years at a time. Talk about well built—they've survived wars, weather, and natural disasters and are still standing today!

STATUE OF LIBERTY

If you start at the base of the statue, you will climb 354 stairs (count 'em) to get to the crown. Whew! Did you know that there is a ladder winding up Liberty's arm leading to the torch? You and I aren't allowed up there. Besides, when it's windy the arm sways up to 5 inches.

Hi, it's me, Jackson. I'm down here, standing as tall as I can! Throughout history, people have been creating structures that tower above them. If something is tall to you, imagine how it looks to a mouse like me!

When Lady Liberty was first erected, she was the tallest manmade structure in the United States. Many buildings in New York City are now much bigger than she is, but none has greater significance for Americans and people all over the world.

Big deal!

What other really big structures can you think of in America and throughout the world? Which ones impress you the most?

You can sit on this full-sized replica of Lady Liberty's foot in the Statue of Liberty. It's as wide as an average pro basketball player is tall, and look at her big toenail! It's about the size of a TV screen. Why isn't her skin green? This is what the whole statue looked like when she was first built, before standing out in the wind and moist air for years.

GLOSSARY

Ancestor—An early member in a family line. For example, your grandmother's grandmother is your ancestor.

Artisan—A skilled worker.

Auction—The public sale of items to the highest bidder (the person who offers the most money).

Colossus—A huge statue or anything gigantic or very powerful.

Cultural heritage—Beliefs and practices associated with a given race or ethnic group that are passed on from generation to generation.

Democracy—A system of government in which the people being governed make the rules they live by. They do this either directly or indirectly by electing representatives who vote on the proposed laws.

Emigrate—To leave one nation or region to live permanently in another.

Frigate—A small warship, originally powered by oars but later by sails and then by modern engines.

Gilded—Covered or highlighted with gold or something of a golden color.

Heirloom—An object of special value that is passed on from generation to generation.

Immigrant—A person who comes to one country from another, intending to live there permanently.

Liberty—The state of being free, having the power to do as one pleases.

Monarchy—A system of government in which a nation is ruled by a king, queen, or emperor.

Monument—A carved statue. Usually meant as a lasting tribute to a notable person or event.

Oppress—To weigh down or crush with the abuse of power or authority.

Patina—A green film that forms on copper and bronze after long exposure.

Pedestal—The base of an upright structure, such as a statue.

Principle—A basic law or accepted rule which serves as a guideline for behavior.

Refugee—Someone who leaves a country to escape danger or persecution.

Rivet—A type of bolt that holds two or more things together.

Salon—A room set aside where people gathered to discuss ideas.

Publisher: Lorie Bacon
Editor: Darcy Ellington
Art Director: Joanne Station
Writers: Clare Meaney, Angela Tripp,
Lorie Bacon, Joanne Station
Illustrator: Jim Harris
Copy Editor: Anne Du Bois
Historical Researcher: Barry Moreno

ACKNOWLEDGMENTS

We would like to acknowledge and thank the following for their assistance and contribution to this book. The help of these individuals and groups has been invaluable: Brad Hill; Barry Moreno and Kevin Daley of the Statue of Liberty National Monument; Marc E. Maurer, Architect; Linda Cable; Wayne Adams; Claire Bacon; Charisse France; Kim Bernard; Julia Laraway; and Linda Muzinich and the first-grade class and Diane Masline and the fifth-grade class, both of Laguna Blanca School.

The wealth of material at the following libraries and archives was indispensable: American Museum of Immigration Library; New York Historical Society; Santa Barbara Public Library; University of California at Santa Barbara.

A special thanks to all of our families who lived through the creation of this book, providing support and thoughtful feedback along the way.

ILLUSTRATION CREDITS

Jim Harris: front cover, 2–13, 15 & 17 (foldouts front and back), 18 top, 21 bottom. Joanne Station: 18 bottom, 20, 22, back cover.

PHOTO CREDITS

Lorie Bacon: 18 top, 20 top left. Battman: 23 left. National Park Service—Statue of Liberty Monument: 19, 20 right, 21. Kevin Daley, NPS: 20 bottom left, 23 right. Printed in Hong Kong.

THE ANSWER PAGE

BRAIN TEASERS ON PAGE 16

1. October 28, 1886.

2. Because copper, if exposed to the elements, develops a greenish film called patina, which changes its color from reddish-brown to green.

3. There are seven points on Liberty's crown, and they represent the seven seas and seven continents.

4. Bedloe's Island.

5. 179,200 lbs. of copper.

6. 305 feet tall.

7. There are 354 stairs in the statue including 142 leading to the observation deck.

8. Emma Lazarus.

9. Gustave Eiffel.

10. 3,000,000.

STICKS, STICKS, STICKS ON PAGE 21

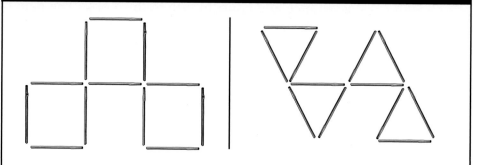

KEEP THE PEACE GAME ON PAGE 18

1. Dog takes mouse.

2. Dog returns alone.

3. Dog takes cat.

4. Dog returns with mouse.

5. Dog takes cheese.

6. Dog returns alone.

7. Dog takes mouse.

For Taryn, Cadence, Quinlan & Henry—our inquisitive mice

TO OUR READERS —

A Home for Lady Liberty is an entertaining and informative exploration of the Statue of Liberty for children. Throughout the book, we have provided the most accurate historical information possible, in both the text and illustrations. The activities are suitable for older children working on their own, as well as for younger children using the book with a parent's help. There is also a glossary to help children with unfamiliar words or concepts. We hope you have fun and learn a lot.

RLibraries™

a division of
Albion Publishing Group
Santa Barbara, CA
(805) 963-6004

Evelyn Hill Group, Inc.
Liberty Island, New York

ISBN 1-880352-57-5
Library of Congress Catalog Number 97-78392